TIME'S PROFILE

THE MACMILLAN COMPANY
NEW YORK . BOSTON . CHICAGO . DALLAS
ATLANTA . SAN FRANCISCO

MACMILLAN & CO., Limited
LONDON . BOMBAY . CALCUTTA
MELBOURNE

THE MACMILLAN COMPANY
OF CANADA, Limited
TORONTO

TIME'S PROFILE

BY
HILDEGARDE FLANNER

Decorations by
FREDERICK MONHOFF

NEW YORK
THE MACMILLAN COMPANY
1929

SET UP BY BROWN BROTHERS LINOTYPERS
PRINTED IN THE UNITED STATES OF AMERICA
BY THE FERRIS PRINTING COMPANY

To F. W. F.
His Memory

Some of these poems are taken from volumes previously published and now out of print, namely: "Young Girl," "This Morning" and "A Tree in Bloom." Acknowledgment is also due to the following magazines: *Poetry, a Magazine of Verse; Palms; The Nation; The Saturday Review; The Overland Monthly.*

CONTENTS

PART ONE

PART TWO

PART THREE

PART FOUR

PART FIVE

PART SIX

PART ONE

A BIRD SINGS AT NIGHT

Who sings upon the pinnacle of night?
   Down, down, unearthly bird, you sing too soon!
O bird, be still!   O bird, the earth is stricken
   To hear you at the bosom of the moon.

Consent to silence and a simple dark;
   Permit the heart to lie within the breast
Unveiled before a thousand memories,
   And in parade salute the loveliest.

Permit the heart, unaltered by your singing,
   To have within the dark its pensive way.
Release the heart amid its joys and sorrows
   Untroubled by what angels have to say.

Unhindered comes the dawn, and you may sing
   Victorious and vocal to the light.
But now delay, and let the heart reverse
   Time's sinister profile on the wall of night.

DUMB

Silence braided her fingers in my hair
And put her ankles close to mine in bed.
She hushed a silver sparrow in his song
And laid against my throat her fragile head.

"I conquered today," she said, "as yesterday,
And now we two shall rest as one tonight.
A girl with silence in her arms,
 (Lie quietly!) is a lovely sight."

And so I rest with silence in my arms,
Her hair across my breath when I would weep.
I cannot even force my tongue to pray
That she will leave me in my sleep.

TO MY BOOKS WHO PERISHED BY FIRE

I have walked where gods were very fair
And Time was but a star below the moon,
Gone up and down the sky with unbound hair,
And home from going far, returned too soon.
Now they are ashes that were once to me
Wings, chariots, wind, journey and resting-place.
Death is too small an urn, and memory
Scarce deep enough to be their burial-vase.
Yet grass will lightly come on these sweet dead
And silence be their loudest requiem,
And while I mourn the ashes I have read,
The striding rain goes marching over them.
Men say that books are learning, but not life.
They were my lovers, who took me to wife.

PHILIPPIAN

"Whatsoever things are lovely"—ah, Saint Paul,
I dare not think on loveliness at all,
For fear I see a face I must not see,
And long for hands that are not stretched to me;
For fear I break a flower and wish a thing
That is not mine for garnering.

"Whatsoever things are lovely . . . think on these."
Oh, bring the eyes to beauty, bend the knees!
Was it a silent or a singing way
That Paul of Ephesus knelt down to pray?
No matter, for all lovely things are pain
To me become Philippian in vain.
Paul, I practise in perverted guise
The word you sent from Rome to make men wise.

TO A TREE IN BLOOM

There is no silence lovelier than the one
That flowers upon a flowering tree at night.
There is no stillness known beneath the sun
That is so strange to bear, nor half so white.
If I had all that silence in my heart,
What yet unfinished heavens I could sing!
My words lift up and tremble to depart,
Then die in air, from too much uttering.
It must have been beneath a tree like this
An angel sought a girl in Galilee,
While she looked up and pondered how the kiss
Of God had come with wings and mystery.
It may be that a single petal fell,
Heavy with sorrow that it could not tell.

DARK MILTON

Dark Milton with his constant nightingale
Sings in the terraces of paradise.
White with listening angels are the skies
And at his side the morning stars unveil.
He sings to harp and thunder, he cries Hail!
Hail, God Almighty blazing in the skies,
Before whose glory (Hail!) death prostrate lies,
And in whose total light the sun is pale.
His word leaps like an eagle on the air,
Reeling sublimely over depths untold,
Hanging above the void where once resounded
Foul upon fouler screaming, even there
Where Satan faltered at the gates of hell, behold
Dark, bright and mighty Milton unconfounded:

DREAD ALOE

I have no dread of loneliness,
Who never knew companionship.
I have no dread of broken heart,
Or severed lip from lip.
This thing I tasted, and this cup
Is but a daily drinking up.

I have no dread of death, for he
Is citizen of low estate
With whom I fraternize but once
And shut outside a marble gate.
Bow once to him and bow no more
In whose dim face we lock the door.

But suddenly to smite the palms
And panic seize the eye,
And heart lie weeping in the breast
With thought of Time let die!
The soul made widow, and remorse
Pacing, pacing by the hearse.

The pain, the anguish and the fire
Of knowing life was spent amiss—
Crucifixion, drowning, hanging
Hold no deeper pang than this.
Regret. Futility. Regret.
That is the dreadest aloe yet.

A POET

Bough that is fresh with manna, break for me!
All of my words lie dead under the tree.
All of my words are down, are lost and fallen,
Too sweet for truth and yet for joy too solemn.
All of my words are dead. I know it well.
Apollo caught the bee and crossed the pollen
With sour dust of a vanished asphodel.
While native honey drips upon the ground
My words break open with an alien sound.
What vacant husbandry is this
To keep an orchard stung by death's black kiss,
To make a garden for the acid briar
And fruit that loosens from a spent desire,
To breed the cactus with its desert pear,
And vision's hollow tree with its dim fare?

I shook the bough, I thought the sun would fall.
But only the sun-forgotten syllable
That throws a little shadow on this page
Fluttered from out the graver foliage,
Only the rind of song a thrush discarded
Fell to my lips unslaked and unrewarded,
Only the salty core of some dry truth
Tasted long since by a diviner youth.
Curse on the flower, curse on the fruit and tree,
Curse on this fallow art, and then curse me!
Oh, for a naked thought to seize the brain
And without gentleness wed in pain!

Oh, for the ecstasy of that stark bed
Where love is quick and no word said,
Where one deep kiss and one sharp cry
Displace the earth beneath the sky,
And looser than descending snow
The melting stars extinguish their own glow,
While Space receives upon his breast
The east crowned with the west.

All things are one.   If I survive that sight
Death will despair of me when I write,
Eloquence will tremble with delight
And glory spring upon me like a hound.
. . . Or I may die and scatter in the night,
No whisper following and no memorial sound.
The waking month will gird his loins with petals,
While over me oblivion sharply settles,
The antlered moon and every thorny star
Will circle upon night's blue calendar,
And quick as ever will the snapping rain
Burst upon the window-pane.
Jesus will tread the lakes of Galilee
Without my foolish wonder or word from me,
And Leda's comely breast support the swan. . . .
For these things will survive when I am gone,
When I am lost undated in the ground
And beauty pairs with glory overhead
And running on the quiet foot of a hound
They cannot wake the dead.

DAILY, FLEET WILDERNESS

Almost is mystery annexed to truth.
  Daily, fleet wilderness, you are overtaken
Almost by rapt pursuer, ah hypnotic youth
  Grown snowy in your wake.   Almost does he
With desperate shadow on your shadow shaken
  Invade and stake you in, O mystery.
Almost the wreath that bears the stars is broken
  And grafted to the wand of arrowy mind,
  The hunt grown hollow, and nothing left to find.

Almost is God shut up within the Book,
  Some other word released to do His acts,
The soul unmiracled, while men evoke
  With passionate chemistry a rational heaven
Builded of constant pillars and deep facts.
  Exiled within a symbol God is driven
While man who made Him classifies His work.
  Nothing remains to mystery but the brink
  Of delicate waters where the deer may drink.

Nothing remains to mystery but man,
  And only as much of him as may survive
Life's scrutiny and death's dismissive yawn.
  Then, then? God's pity! Give us God once more!
He only knows if any of us live
  When the door shuts and the seal is on the door.
Forgetting and denying we may strive
  The old corrosive riddle to erase.
Ever it burns more crimson in its place.

Return, fleet wilderness, for man is ready now.
Cover him, mystery, with your delphic bough.
Into the unbegotten he has fled.
Daily, fleet wilderness, you claim the dead.

HOUSE BELOW THE DEW

Not the open bird upon the sky, nor the single moon,
  Nor the nodding butterfly,
Nor lissom wheat, nor cold creature the snake
  Ever looks Time in the eye.
Moon is a dial, only a silver slate
  Where Time counts another night.
Amorous and unthinking, cats play below
  And hiss by that light.
Hearing spring's fiddle in the grass, or the wands of ice,
  A butterfly may come and go.
The bitter drums of Time and his wheels' black scar
  She does not know.
Prompt on the bough both flower and bird arrive and
      settle
  In April, that green land,
And lambs in white curls throng the world, unheeding
  The furious tremble of Time's nervous hand.
What flower, what beast, what tree or roaming beetle
  Has ever cared or understood
That Time is more than a petal snowing to be gone
  Or a dim lassitude?
Though summer speaks a hundred tongues
  She leaves Time untranslated.
Her story runs from ivory freesia to the darkest fig,
  Signed in honey but undated.
Even the rock, the lean and lonely, who is twin of Time
  Reckons not from his own birth
But, frozen to his secret, locks upon his breast
  The skeleton of earth.

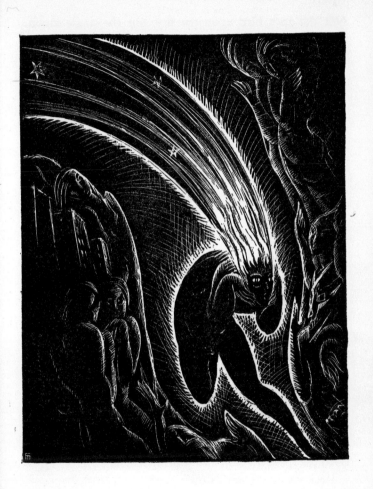

No, not the rock, no, not the flower riding on the bough
    Ever looks in Time's face,
Or knows what strata of the sky, what dizzy pollen
       made him
    Or what race
    Sired by Space.
Man only (listen), yes, man only, man whose flesh
    Unfolds less strangely than the rose
And in whose breast a spirit flies more various than a
       bird—
    Man knows, only man knows!
He puts his petty brow to that vast eye,
    Looks and does not fall in,
But bears in his heart the age of earth,
    The stars and all their kin—
Bears in his brain a comet, yet staggers not, not he!
    Look up! Look at the sky!
Behold the blazing ciphers
    Man measures Time by.
Listen—how many vigorous clocks
    Clucking on the wall
Reduce the father of all life
    To an interval.
Observe how man, colossal dwarf,
    With celebrated pain
Confines him to the whisper of a watch
    And wears him on a chain.
Hark! The chimes are tugging at the steeple
    And knock another day out of the sun.
Man needs this ceremony for his rising
    Though birds with bells want none.

Up, man! Up, mite! Up, king of earth!
  Day was made for you,
The virgin sky and the unmated earth,
  These too.
You who hold the towers of life and death,
  What is Time to you?—
Time, that meagre scaffolding to build
  A house below the dew.

A LETTER TO D. E.

Dear Sir: I never wrote to you who wrote to me,
And you, while I delayed my note, turned to the moon,
Ceased, ceased to be, God knows, forsook your shadow,
East, east and west, it trails the earth no more.
I never saw your face or heard your voice
Save here on the open page, word, bird and arrow
Sprung in flight ironic up the empty curve of day.
I know not where you rest, what season turns its dial
          of hyacinth,
Its disk of snow and ice across your muted breast,
What local dust grows subtle with your name,
Or if they gave your ashes to the wind, and you fled up
Intent upon a finer star than this.

Referring to that dark event you passed, sir,
We all will overtake you, one by one,
Loosen, alas, the sandal and give up the race,
Abandon the horizon and come in to that renowned
Abiding-place called death.   Sleep, little one, sleep.

It is not so!   Tell me it is not so!
It's not too deep to waken, nor yet so silent that it will
          not break,
Nor yet so ultimate no syllable can fall
Down, down the wall, no bright leaf flutter and no
          tear be shaken.
Tell me the dead awaken, sentient still, upon the ivory
          hill

Of heaven. Tell me they still know earth and her fair
        almanac,
The snowy moon that lifts her shoulder to the
        night,
The slipping rain that breaks upon the ground,
The freesia settled lightly on her stem.
Can you forget, O dead, the fields of home,
The way you went, the glossy waters that you stood
        beside,
The phantom wheat your feet returned among?
Can you forget the great eyes of your love
Upturned to yours and undenying?
The heart undone like a magnolia flower, the hovering
        face?
Can you forget how joy leaped on your breast,
How sorrow lay there like a fallen monument,
How man, in black vast moments, knows he is
        alone,
And seeks with agony to look in his own eyes?

Can you forget—but who knows, no, not I,
And you, dear sir, whether your gaze is empty of the
        world,
Whether your fingers yearn to ease their immortality
Within a mortal hand just out of reach, or on earth's
        first returning crocus,
Who, who am I to peck your silence with my feverish
        questioning
Now you are gone to quiet inviolate?

Farewell, until the night I overtake you.
Farewell, until our circling shadows overlap
And I may read the answer you can never give.
Farewell.   I write these words in shifting brook-water,
I hang my letter on a branch of wind.

ASCENT

This is the sky, the bottomless and bitter air, the void
      where space alone has foothold,
This, this, immensity without a fence, a bar, a wisp to
      catch
  You if you fall.
This is the floating wilderness, the unfettered air, heaven
      revolving intolerably
  On the point of my heart's beat.
Here only the rootless wind can flourish and die, the
      light unfold and wither to darkness,
  The little bird choke and spin,
  While man
  Butting his forehead on infinity
Leans, gapes and plunges fainting into
  The echoless and empty chasm of time.

This is the sky, never impounded by pushing angels,
      never reduced to blocks of paradise
For Almighty God's heel of loud flame to burn on.
  No never.
Never the least thing clings or clots here, makes acres or
      vacant
  Angles or printed dust,
Never the smallest spider hangs her elastic couch on any
  Airy thorn—
But glittering space broods on itself, upright, without
      support
  And without effort.

O terrible chastity, wherein the mind of man finds no
     obstruction
   And no help.

PART TWO

GOD PITY THEM

God pity them who have no love
  To lie beside and touch or kiss.
Rather be lost and lowly under,
  Rather be dead than know not this.

God pity them and stop their tears
  Who had a love and buried it.
Rather be darkness and no morning,
  Than candle with the flame unlit.

God pity them who tarry after
  Beside the gate where love went through.
God pity them when love has failed them,
  And life has failed them too.

TO ONE WHO UNDERSTANDS

There are too many things I must not say.
I think if I should see you, on that day
A sharp, amazing silence would surprise
All questions from my lips and from my eyes,
While memory would sit and tear apart
The tense and screaming fibres of my heart.

There was a time when you and I could spell
The silence into love, and it was well.
But now, if we should meet, I would go dumb
And you would cease to talk, and it would come—
A different silence, yes, a piteous thing,
A little creature, starved and quivering,
We could not feed with words, could not release
Its unsaid being into spoken peace.

Then you might take my hand and let it fall
Back to my side. . . . That would be all.
I know that I would sob and turn away. . . .
There are too many things I could not say.

INTERVAL

Now the storm is weary.
Let it rest.
Like a woman under weeping,
Let it rest.
Like a runner sick of swiftness,
Let it rest.
Like a pain weary of flesh,
Let it rest.

But my heart
That turns and cries
Above the fire your memory makes in me

Can find no rest
No rest.

CIRCLE

Of all the motions I have made,
One forms in endless grace—
My hands uplifted whitely
To your face.

Of all the sounds that I have heard,
One cannot sink to rest—
Your footstep going east,
Mine going west.

A WREATH FOR ASHES

I.

Unsung, unsigned upon the dust of time,
   Shall we sink down, we two, and sift together,
My song forgotten, and your lovely page
   Blank in eternity's effacing weather?

Will the rain waver, and the vacant snow
   Replace the beauty of a path we trod,
And the wind rustle and slip over us,
   Lost between stars upon our way to God?

How tragic anger, then, how futile hate,
   When two dazed atoms, wafted out of sight,
Vainly recall that such a thing as love
   Existed this side of eternal night.

II.

I am bereft of any word to utter.
   Here on my lips no syllable is heard.
Look in my face—I have no word to give you.
   Look in my eyes—I am widow to a word.

Of what avail to write a thousand poems
   Or in love's history assume a part,
When every stroke of pen can only bury
   Deeper the dead word in the sorrowing heart?

III.

I know a wound that closes to the eye,
    Retreats from view and leaves no mark behind.
Sorrow has worn it smooth, but far beneath
    It sets a flaming circle on the mind.

There is a wound that disappears at last
    And one may say, "Observe that I am whole."
But where no eye can see, no stranger guess,
    It bleeds indelibly upon the soul.

IV.

I said farewell.   I did.   But did I say it?
    I said it.   Farewell.   Did I say that word?
Yes, no.   Incredible.   Recorded, done.
    Yes, I have said it.   Yes, and you have heard.

Well, I have said it then—my mouth has said it,
    And I will stay by it, if one must stay.
But I, not I had any part in it.
    I merely uttered what my lips must say.

You said it, you!   Your wish invoked the sound.
    You struck that thought as if it were a bell,
And in my heart, three thousand miles away,
    With instant art you rang the word farewell.

V.

When winter throws himself on summer's breast
    And there begets dim snow and bitter hail,
May you remember how the fields of home
    Are sweet with lupin and the song of quail.

May you remember how the hills flow up
    In lakes of emerald above the world,
And on the slope and crest of every billow
    Armadas of the poppy sail unfurled.

May you remember how the morning air
    Shines as if the sun were standing still,
And natural as flowers in the grass
    A man may see a god upon the hill.

May you remember how the meadow-lark
    Shakes and breaks his song against the light,
And how the laurel-shadow softly paces
    Around the laurel tree from dawn to night.

When winter runs aloft his sombre column
    To fly the tattered snow and ragged sleet,
May you remember how another winter
    Let up a host of freesias to your feet.

HOW MYSTICAL MY FLESH

How mystical my flesh and without fire. . . .
O love, I lie as snow upon your heart.
Circle me not with fierce arms, for desire
Has in me no abiding, and no part.
Doves shall become a bitter thing to me,
Before I tire of them and send them hence.
If mine the fault, then mine the sorrow be,
Cherishing fear, naming it innocence.
In some dim meadow let us softly weep,
Holding delicate hands, and smile, and rest.
But oh, will not that you should turn to sleep
Beside this body or upon this breast.
Our hearts will break, mayhap, nor find a home. . . .
Poor pilgrims dying, on the way to Rome.

SONNETS IN QUAKER LANGUAGE

I.

Thee is obscured, beloved, as though I
Beheld thy body through a ghost between.
What death of other lovers, and what cry
Of other deaths and loves here intervene?
Is it thee carries, like old ambergris,
The sweet, tenacious presence of the dead,
That, like a wind about us, memory
Disturbs the dust thee once thought buriéd?
Or is it I who veil a wakeful ghost
Within the haunted distance of my eyes,
And am forever the unearthly host
Unto a thing long dead that never dies?
Thee kiss me through a ghost! and so inter
All past loves in a radiant sepulchre.

II.

Thee sets a bell to swinging in my soul,
And though the sound is nebulous and dark,
Yet musical my thought unto its toll,
And seldom is my hush! and loud my hark!
Thee knows that in response continual
My heart is all ways resonant to thee,
Yet with how dim a sound antiphonal,
Like a lost wind that blows beneath the sea.
Can thee resolve confusion of my tears
Into a single silence of desire?
Can thee, when singing has gone cold with fears,
Put on more music and put on more fire?
If so, then I am cloister to a bell
That utters advent of a miracle.

III.

Spring is the very disenchanted time
When I must tell thee what I do not know;
When thee would summon up my heart to rhyme
Its beating upon yes or upon no.
But all the while I look between thy eyes
And dare not touch the candle of my gaze
Unto the deep fire that within thee lies,
(Still after death will there be yeas and nays?).
And all the while desire and yet restrain
Our hands confederate in ecstasy,
And one last moment to evade my pain
Say lightly, "It is spring today. . . . Oh see
How Proserpine beneath her zone discloses
Her April body made of naked roses."

IV.

When thee is weary of the earth and all
The summers of a printed calendar;
When thee would hinder the continual
Arrival of to-morrow as before;
When both thy heart and spirit are as stone,
Gone rigid and grown terrible in thee;
When life seems preterit and death alone
The only creature left—thee come to me.
There will be slumber for thee in my heart,
When I have smiled at thee and dimmed the candles,
And toward dawn as darkness falls apart
We will arise to hunt in dewy sandals
The pale wild deer that has a lacy horn
And lives on hidden manna and star corn.

V.

Unto the low sweet solace of the grass
Let me rehearse my heart's due observation
That love and lover's patience fail and pass,
That flame and taper are not one creation,
That night both antedates and follows morn,
And wisdom has her days of less degree.
Not loudly, but remotely and forlorn
This grievance I commit to grass—how thee
Impales me flower by flower on such a pang
That petal after pollen down is shaken.
To-morrow comes no foliage to hang
The bough from which to-day the buds are taken.
Behold, upon the grass my heart is bowed,
Accusing thee before an emerald crowd.

VI.

Hearing a sound that may be thy return,
I set my heart upon the window sill.
By such a mortal lamp thee may discern
The tossing pathway on the hidden hill.
The leaves are stepping softly from the trees.
I listen.   That was a bird sighed in her nest.
I lean and wonder if thee runs and sees
The lighted dream upon the dreamer's breast.
But no foot springs upon the silken air,
No strand of silence breaks to let thee by.
Thee does not come.   But still I wait and stare
Then turn from the massive darkness with a cry.
For now the desolate owl with lonely shout
Descends the mountain and my light goes out.

VII.

I know not where thee sleeps to-night, my love.
"Far up into the mountain," so thee said.
I only know some purple height above
Is the moon's camping-ground and thy cool bed.
Elate upon dark altitude thee lies
With the abundant sky spread over thee.
The stars are multiplied within thy eyes,
The sum of night reduced to filigree.
My heart has followed thee and should thee hear
A little step ascend the wilderness
It is perhaps the light boot of the deer,
Or should it stumble thee can surely guess.
May thee be folded from all mountain harm
And dream of waking upon love's quiet arm.

SKY MEETING

Alone on the mountain ridge I waited, waited.
Immensity plunged to the sky and fainted
In its inverted ocean of gentian-burning,
Collapsed in cobalt whirls and circled
Into the high suspended lakes of air.
Below my feet the wilderness let down
From spire to spire; fell, hurled, swept, swooned
And with the pendant waters loosened from the snow
   Finished falling.
Finished? no not until the vast descent
Jarred up and tripped upon
The lower hills with hyacinth backs
And over these sprawled flying, flung face
   Down.   This is the desert.

Below my feet, with balm sealed, honey-locked,
The trees are rooted in velocity.
Slow from the breast of rock they take their life
And inch by inch put green into the sky.
Sloping below them pillars of blue snow
Fall as the sun moves on.

I am waiting alone in the steeple of the world.
Where have you wandered on the spacious snow,
Where bent to peer into infinity
   And there slipped in,
Where stood to lean on the amber body of a pine?
Here no bird speaks, no little prophet dares

To prick the round air with a song.
Here in the icy wilderness I am alone,
Alone in the centre of the looping wind,
Throwing his rings about me, closer coiling,
Until I can almost see the wind that binds,
Seeing the fir tree spin between his crystal sides,
Until I fear I too will spin
Wound in a spring of winding and unwinding wind
And shoot in stars of bitter snow
   Into the quiet Mojave.

But suddenly through the maze of storm
You run and come to find me,
Stumbling to rest with a cry at my feet. . . .

And we go down to the canyon, down from the wind,
Down from inhuman pinnacles and towers of space,
Back to the shallow bells in the brook's heart,
   Back to earth,
Counting the sumless snow which is
   Love's number.

CRYSTAL NIGHT

This is the crystal, the mirror of night,
   When moon leans over her own serene image
And upon earth a light is born,
   Love, on your heart a light arises,
A slow intense abiding light
Of brightness facing brightness.

Who chants in the garden, what lithe bird,
   And whose throat sweetens at the throat of night
While you at my shoulder gleaming
   Reflect on me
   The ineffable brightness of the brooding air?

SERENADE

Evening passed us on a balmy foot
  Slowly.
After dusk the jerking moth and the tidal dark.
Earth upon her shoulder takes the night,
The stars have opened and their light comes down,
While at the roadside walks the glittering cat.
  Sleep, beloved.

Life's meaning runs away like falling water.
There goes the answer and is lost at sea.
  Tell me, beloved.
Though day was broken, now the night is ours,
  In sleep,
Healed breast to breast of distance and desire—
O undivided and anointing night
Whose universal couch is spread for two.

SONNET

We have a thousand deaths to die each day.
Death by little death we kill each hour,
Time by frosty time we blast the flower
That in a finer world would have its way.
Laugh and talk as loudly as they may
A million tongues have neither joy nor power,
Upon a million tongues the grape is sour,
The song is futile and the word is nay.
Beloved, when I think how Life is thrown,
Magnificent in man's unwary face,
And see the farthing he has wit to hold—
Beloved, take me to a better place,
A little nearer to your heart, alone,
To put away a coin of living gold.

AVOWAL

How can we be what we were before?
How flee backward through a shut door?
How push the rose down into her stem,
Or signal the hot stars and reverse them?
How can we stop now?   How restore
The plushy blossom to the lean core?
Say it, say it again.   How unravel
On the spider's foot her lacy travel?
Whisper it, for my heart is shaken,
Where is the dream, if the dreamer waken?

How can I stand where I once stood,
A child, enchanted, in the ferny wood?
Me, slim and credulous, the wind leaping to
Fashioned in his image with a thumb of dew.
Me, quiet as marble and stiff with delight
The brook anointed with bright brown light.

How can we go back, how retrace
Years, tears, flesh (blood stumbling) to this place,
And lie down, fall, sink in one piece
(Not leaf-limb divided) deep down into peace?
I was a child once, and that was best,
Bounding like a fountain, then falling to rest,
Flying a kite and climbing after
Into the sky's indigo rafter,
Staring clairvoyant at a tree
Because I heard it speak to me,
Or freezing into wonder where
A green moth tottered on the air.

That was best, yes, to walk in the pied wood,
My sandal in my hand, and my foot
Bright and simple on the moss. . . . And yet
Would I go back, would I return
To unconverted void, would I unburn
What once was blaze and now is ash
And run darkly by light of a false wish?
Would I resolve my sum of flesh and bone
And me, the fluttering half of the equation
Back to equal mystery and its evasion?
No. . . . For when I remember love I am undone,
Yes, split like a shadow in the sun,
Yes, beating in my blood, snared and broken,
Thinking, when love spoke, had I not spoken,
Had I not come ahead, had I still haunted
Dream's deep labyrinth and the enchanted
Dim tilted woods I remembered, I wanted.

No, give me this instead, this steep crown
No child ever reached to or pulled down.
No, give me this instead, bind me and tether
Fast in love's raiment and his million-mesh—
Then throw me to the years and let them go!
I vow in their very shadow still to gather
An incorporeal rose from summer's flesh
Winter cannot wither with slow snow!

SONNET

Spirit to spirit struggles luminous
And intermingles in the body's kiss.
Ever the flesh, alert and glorious,
Profits by such an advocate as this.
Ever the whispering flesh at this event
For which it softly smoldered in delight
Breaks into falling stars that press and faint
Into the steepest circle of the night.
Slow from the lap of love the body turns
Meeker from plunging into paradise,
While at the body's edge the spirit burns
Bright as a mirror that drinks down the skies,
Hoarding the passing light of man's embrace,
Shedding it back again into his face.

PART THREE

SINGING

There is not a dead man even
Could lie still,
Spring, when you begin to strike
Harps upon the hill.

On the earth and under it,
Along a mighty street,
The quick and dead run up to kiss
The flowers between your feet.

PACIFIC WINTER

The quietly sipping rain that sucks the rose
Dangles from a cloud and then is gone.
The mists bow low and falling prone disclose
Towers and cities made of violet stone.
The air with one quick flash is lit within
And every flower is limpid on her stem
And crystal bushes shudder and begin
To disengage their rainbows gem from gem.
The trees look downward from green galleries
And view the garden with a plumy nod,
While I in vain with dim and spinning eyes
Run to outrun the presence of a god
Who paused an instant here and left behind
His fugitive cameo upon my mind.

WHITE MAGNOLIA BLOSSOM

The rolling, staggering bee, the honey-fronted,
Shoves his gypsy face into the pollen,
Thrusts and wallows with delight unblunted
While over him the yellow snow has fallen
And under him the stamens deeply shaken
Tremble. Tumult, O bee—in her cool tower
Sleeps perfection that no fire can waken,
Slumbers, alaska-white, who said a flower,
Who said a more than flower, who can discern
What lantern-like and secret single
Word is bright enough for her but will not burn,
What sound is pure enough to hold and mingle
With this unseizable, impending doom—
To fall unfathomably into beauty's bloom?

QUIETLY, SUDDENLY

The grass peers from the ground in sweet amaze
To see the flitting ankles of the rain,
And pigmy-lilies spring where they have lain
To open on the world a minute gaze.
The plainest bird grows elegant with praise,
The stillest bird lifts up his flute again,
And linnets publicly recite the old refrain
Persuaded that they utter roundelays.
The ways of joy and life since life began
Rehearse in every bird that shouts and flies,
Repeat in every flower that storms the earth,
Until at last the darkened son of man
Awakes in festival and loudly cries,
God's only daughter, Spring, has come to birth!

SUMMER GOES

The sound of summer slipping from the trees
Is scarcely heard in this bright land.
The heavy fig-leaves falling to the ground
Make a nearly summerless and yellow sound,

But the pearly tree filled up with linnets
Soft as roses on the marble twig
Dismisses summer only to invite
A snowless winter to its arms of white.

And winter comes, with her unsleeping flowers.
Or is it spring that flashes and is here?
Or is it both lie dreaming in one place
And rise bewildered, face to face?

HARVEST

Every sparrow at his pleasure
Quaffs the grapes to-day.
Bees and linnets drink the plums
And throw the cups away.

August is upon us now
In her yellow sandal.
What she gives she takes again.
Goddess, vandal.

If within my heart no harvest
Shines nor any reaping
Glimmers ready for the scythe,
August, here is weeping.

Others gather violet
Figs and heavy fruit.
Others gather, others give.
I am destitute.

May the laughing oriole,
May the whispering linnet
Share my vine and welcome to
Any sweetness in it.

For there is no other
Person but a bird
I could offer honey to
Or a mellow word.

SUMMER HILLS

Here summer has an amber palace
After winter's emerald.
Hills are made of yellow glass,
Meadows glimmer and what was
Green and beryl to behold
Falls to dust and pallid amber.

Under earth the water slumbers
Secret as a ghost.
Weather glows in saffron embers,
Lupins drop to golden cinders
And the place thereof is lost,
Lost the rush and whisper of fair water.

Summer's lonely domes are disenchanted
Of every flower and banner spring let fly,
Of all the misty loveliness of winter.
Only light is left, and it is haunted.

STORM

The lofty wind is beating at the hill's dark breast
And in the face of heaven springs the storm.
Night wheels and stumbles like a wounded beast,
Rears up and plunges in alarm
And knocks the shaken sky from east to west.

The mountain wind is blowing his melancholy horn
And fierce upon his music flies the rain.
The clamorous wet rocks are crying, Storm!
And there the monster rages and proclaims
That he was god before all other gods were born.

THE OWL

The sweet and ghostly laughter of the owl
Last night shook upward from the light bamboo.
The garden rose and trembled at the sound,
Suspended in enchantment and in dew.
What strange reversal of the blood and soul,
What dizzy floating upward from the earth,
When suddenly the darkness broke in two
Upon the honeyed edge of this soft mirth,
And in its wake a glint of mockery
Unbearable to hearts worn out with prayer.
For man, asleep, still labours over fears
The dreamless owl abandons to the air.

THE RAIN

The rain upon the earth falls down
Long and naked, straight and wan;
Still and white along the hill,
Bending to her miracle,
Slow and silver in the grass—
Lover, maid and sorceress.
She lays a yellow jasmine blossom
In the centre of her bosom,
Leaps and flutters like a moth
When the wind is from the south,
Bows and murmurs like a fountain
When the wind is from the mountain.
Have me now—oh, take me, love,
She sighs along the orange grove.
To every flower, even the least,
Sister, take me on your breast!
To every vine and every tree,
Leafy fellow, pity me!
I am the daughter of the storm—
Let me rest upon your arm.
I am come from paradise—
Let me rest upon your thighs.
I am young, but I am weary,
My time is come to perish, nearly.

Love me, have me, for the dust
Takes me unto him at last.
Take me, have me, ere the wind
Drives me to horizon end.

I am the rain, I am the rain—
Take me to your arms again!

Pale and naked, straight and wan,
She is falling to the ground.
Tree nor vine can lift her up,
She is falling, she will slip.
Lilac's love nor rose's shoulder
Can detain her or can hold her.
With a long sigh in the mist
She is falling, she is lost.

Sob and whisper, cry in vain—
I am the rain, I am the rain!

OCTOBER NIGHT

The moonlight is of glass among the trees,
Elate and cool among the haunted trees.
Night is detained in delicate light, in lunar tapers,
So fair and final is the night, complete as stone.
Here is summer's frosty ghost and her pale skeleton.
Night, the luminous tomb, contains the remembered
      sleeper

While bird in olive orchard
Hangs bells along the orchard
And shakes the lighted branches to his belated vesper.
Like syllables of prophecy spoken from a star
The song abounds and lingers on the air
Till silence, as a mighty door, shuts on a holy whisper.

UNCREATURED

I wish I were ghost-walking in the snow-feathered rain,
   Stepping like a phantom in the mountain height.
The snow would follow me and fill up my footprints,
   Leaving them not human, and full of soft light.

The yucca of spun ice, the frost like silver pollen,
   And the snow's white blossom falling on the stone
Snare me with strangeness, drift me with silence,
   And anything I ever did, lies undone.

It is good to be a wraith once, good to be uncreatured,
   Walking in a world that is pale as hellebore.
But if the sun were suddenly to smite me on the fore-
      head
   I would go down to earth again, real once more.

THIS, THE BRIGHT SKY

This, the bright sky bending on the earth,
Strikes with scriptural light the lapis mountain,
Falls and blazes with a stroke of splendour,
Shoots and pulses in the blood and brain,
Till brain and blood together swoon in light
And shine fraternal through the maddened eye.

No moon his, all stars put out,
Man, extinguished in his own wide gaze,
Frantic, searching for the word that merges
Him with the aloof tense lustre,
Loud into the glowing air at last
Cries with despair and joy, *I too am here!*

HILLS

I know hills whose trees confess
A passion for the wilderness,
Whose pagan utterance of early spring
Swells down the canyon paths to bring
A palinode of winter's heresy,
Whose silent attitude of revelry
Invites from day to day all those who pass
To heathen baptism in waves of grass.

YOUNG EUCALYPTUS

Here in this vertical, wan place
    Of girl-like trees
    There are three sounds.
One, of water shaken softly
    Underground.
One, of mystery discreetly moving
    Through the grass.
And one
    A creature with a hidden throat
    No man may ever hear.

AFTER A WINTER RAIN

God said, "Look out now, there's a girl,"
    And the mountain halted,
Lifted her lupins to her knees
    And retired insulted.

Thus Sierra Madre does
    In this glassy weather,
When granite heights and flowered hills
    Invade the town together.

FAIRY UNDER THE BAMBOO TREE

She has a crystal foot.   She walks
   In a gossamer shoe,
Hither-yonder, shadow of
   A leaf upon a leaf.
She has a little harp,
   Hush, wind!   Listen, linnet!
The toad takes out his jewel
   If she but pass,
The moth lets down his sail
   To wait her coming.

   O dainty ghost
   Whose radiant fingers twinkle
   Gavottes for mice and men
   Under the bamboo shadow.

WIND'S BRIDE

O fervent wind
   wind's fervor,
   parting the swinging curtains of the pepper-tree
      to rush in
      to lie down
      singing.

Only bright vacancy inside.
This is the wind's bride.

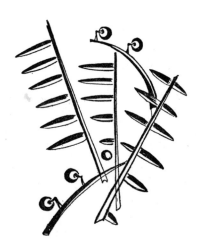

MOMENT

I saw a young deer standing
Among the languid ferns.
Suddenly he ran—
And his going was absolute,
Like the shattering of icicles
In the wind.

TREES

Pale grey and yellow limbs,
That never move
But step unceasingly in beauty,
You have come to me,
And all my thoughts are as a forest
With crystal-feathered birds.

THE RAIN IS BRAVE

The rain does not fumble.
　　She comes down straight,
With lustre-precision
　　Concluding fate.
One leap from the sky,
　　One lunge at the ground,
One instant only
　　Of fractured sound—
Identity's ended.
　　It was for this
The deep, suicidal
　　Dive of bliss,
The single signature
　　On the grass,
That says *it is I*
　　And that means *alas*.

DESERT MORNING

Everything is stiff and sparkling,
    Everything is still—
Not a tremor, yet creation
    Spinning like a wheel
Polishes the rim of heaven,
    Clamps the earth in sight,
Paves the desert with a yellow
    Glaze of solid light.
Coming winter, coming spring,
    I am here to wonder
How a staff of lilies can
    Break hard gold asunder.

LILAC IN THE ARROYO

Lilac of the wilderness,
Sweet plumage of the spring,
Spread over me your wings,
   (Soft give me shelter, lilac)
While childish February
   Puts on, takes off
   The slippers of the rain.

THE SNAIL

Not without dignity the lumbering snail
All through the owly night goes down the walk,
Slanting her wanded eyes, leaving a trail
And bearing her cottage curled upon her back.
So slow, so soft, so hated, now she goes
To curve her viscous lip and cling and eat,
Gorging her fill on rhubarb and on rose
And many a perfume-cup and salad sweet.
Her waving eyes, her gait, her gluey kiss
Slide upon the garden's helpless cheek.
Beauty, without a cry, falls prey to this,
An enemy so tardy and so meek
Who shrinks beneath a log at the first warning
Of the printless, bootless, weightless heel of morning.

BURIAL OF THE MOCKING-BIRD

Underneath pomegranate bush
(This way sob and this way hush)
Lay him in his little feathers
Where the coral foliage gathers.
Here the lilies of December
Light his slumber with small amber
Lanterns lifted at his head.
Oh, lament the song he had!
Mute he lies, once musical.
Who saw falter, or saw fall?
Airy feet are now detained
Far from moonlight and from wind.
Flickering wings have gone the last
Flight a wing goes.   He is dust.
Amen.   Amen.   How lost, how still is
He among the winter-lilies.

CLEAR DAY OF WIND

On such a day as this
    the mountains stalk the town,
    ponderous in menace,
    terrible and brown.
    Calamity restrained by
    a gossamer device
    lours and topples over us
    from the rigid skies.
    Threaten. Coming nearer.
    Have hope left? One step more.
    Lost! the mountains back of us,
    Pacific lies before!
    And the writhing, snapping wind,
    a devil like a god,
    whips the mountains on again
    if they nod.

DAWN ON THE DESERT

Day on dewless hinges
    Swings open, and the night
Loosened from receding stars
    Falls sideways out of sight.

The mountains bestride vastness
    And immensity cleaves apart,
Split in two by silence
    Expanding in its heart.

One crow with his obsidian oar
    Rows along the sky.
Moored only to himself he drifts
    Upon eternity,

While far below I stand and put
    My hand across my face
For fear I shout and leap into
    The bright abyss of space.

SUPERIOR PEOPLE

The humming-bird unwinds before the fuchsia.
  His little emerald engine never misses.
The sparrow at his shopping in the grass
  Peers among the poppy's yellow dishes.

The thrush, whose legs run under him like spokes,
  Wheels with amber frown about his business,
And the deliberate snail with roof and rental
  Removes from pansy to the new hibiscus.

The dove that kneels and murmurs on the bough
  Blows a honey-bubble from her throat.
With a sweet stutter then she flies away
  Leaving the ample day vague and remote.

THE HEART TURNS EASTWARD

(*Written in California*)

In alien yellow grass, alas, poor heart,
Come the slow feet, and you are dumb with memory
Of amethyst orchard clover, brimming clover,
Dark bowls where the sweet bee stumbles,
Clear fragrant grass that flows
Up to the knee with June's deep whisper,
Poor heart, come home!

Laugh in your mountain, quail with the curled horn,
My friend was a bob-white with a lovely whistle,
Laugh alas, laugh alas!
My friend was an old house set in an orchard,
My friend was a street where I walked with my love,
My friend was the city where my children were born,
Laugh alas, miles away, years away,
Where the dark bee stumbles in the deep evening
And close on his heels the fire-flies sparkle.

Let me go home again!
   I am coming—
I am sick of walking in gold alien grass.
   I am coming—
Sick for the lilac's sweet cornucopia,
Sick for a brook that skips like a child,
Laughs like a child in familiar meadows,
Sick for my own land where rain comes in summer
With dew in her fingers and bells on her feet,

Where autumn dances and winter is still,
Where roses mount the appointed stem
And soberly leave when they should.
I am lonely here among flowers that are strangers.
Give me one flower that smells of home
And stares like a neighbour.
Give me a maple with robins in it.
Take your Spanish acres and deserts of opal!

Let me go home from the heavy ocean,
Let me go home from the burning mountains,
Wading with slow feet sunk in memory,
Deep in June's whisper, coming, coming,
Up to the heart in bright scented rain—

    This is my land!
    Here is my home,
    There the door opens—
    Come in, beloved! . . . *Where have you been?*

DICTIONARY

O sassafras, your portrait in a book
Has made the letter S a pitcher of dew,
Has made the years fall open at the blessings,
And cut time's alphabet in two.

And there are no more words words, only
A piece of woodland coined with sun-in-dapple
And near my foot the three-times trillium leaf
And under her parasol the pale May-apple.

And I am standing halved by past and present,
Confused in light that's double like a shell,
Recalling the hermit thrush, his fine soprano
And that no other bird could hide so well,

Recalling maiden-hair in frail triangles,
And a little snake who had a yellow chin,
And Judas-tree with green hearts hung, so choicely,
And next year's beads of roses tight within.

O sassafras, your portrait in a book
Has left my mind half-slanted and awry,
Tilted to eastward in a western land
To see the wind-flower tremble and hear the whip-
        poor-will cry.

PART FOUR

GIRL TO A UNICORN

Lighter than a branch of lilies
  Falling among grasses
  Is the falling of thy hoof-beat
  As thee passes.

I have heard that thee will suffer
  Only a chaste girl
  To touch her finger (touching lightly)
  To thy horn of pearl.

Virgins (and these only)
  Slip near enough to see,
  Bearing in their quiet eyes
  The hush of chastity.

Will thee hearken, Unicorn,
  Hover at my call,
  Pause and let me stride thee,
  Angel-animal?

  Ah, never did Europa,
    Lovely on a bull,
      Have a steed so lissom
      Or so beautiful!

DAPHNE

They told her she had hair the colour
Of a nightingale.
They told her that her eyes were candles
Lit beneath a veil.

They praised her feet like narrow doves
Mated on the floor,
Saying there were never feet
Like her feet before.

They praised her shining voice that rang
Like stars dropped in a glass.
"Sing to thy little yellow shell!"
And so the night would pass.

But when they came too near to her
And touched her with the hand,
She drew her hair across her eyes.
She could not understand.

And when they said a thing to her
That she had never heard,
Her heart plunged into silence there
Like a hunted bird.

She caught her violet mantle close,
The Tyrian upon the white;
She quivered like a little twig;
She stepped into the night.

They called her name within the dark,
They searched beneath the sun,
But there was not a broken flower
To show where she had run.

Everything was very still,
Far too still, they said.
So they turned and went away,
Unaccompanied.

Nothing moved where they had sought,
Nothing sang or wept.
Beneath a tree that had no name,
Silence turned and slept.

TWO POEMS FOR AN UNBELIEVING CHILD

I.

One day I met a fairy
Walking in the rain,
Holding up her foggy wings,
Tripping on her train.

We took a deep look
At each other there.
I saw her eyes were desolate
Beneath her tasseled hair.

And I could have sobbed aloud
In the stumbling rain
To see across a fairy's mouth
Such a smile of pain,

To see her in the pointed grass
Falter toward me,
As if she sought to break her grief
In frail proximity.

But between the thought of weeping
And the falling of a tear
She proudly turned and walked away
Behind an iris spear.

If I could only comfort her,
Could soothe away the pain
Of that creature like a stamen
Walking in the rain.

II.

Silence fluttered at me like a moth,
As if my soul and body were alight.
Silence withdrew and something staid,
Something with the quietest name.

An almost-angel nearly dawned on me.

WORDS FOR UNHEARD MUSIC

Some say that there are flowers
Along the paths of hell,
Trillia lamenting
And bent asphodel.

Shimmering, long lilies,
White, abandoned things,
With only white companions
To their sorrowings.

There is that about them
When they gleam and sway,
Maketh even Proserpine
Turn her head away,

Maketh even death himself
Go a pace apart,
Troubled by a frail song
Lifting in his heart.

And the lilies tremble,
And the asphodel,
Like nocturnal moths
Along the paths of hell.

PORTRAIT OF A STRANGE WOMAN

Far after her without a leaf of sound,
Her dress falls like a hush upon the ground.

She wavers like a cherry-spray
And strangely hesitates away,

And she is gone again . . . who goes
Where I know not, and no one knows.

Where has she fled upon her (unseen) feet
With steps invisible and indiscreet?

Where does she pause to rest, and where
Shake out the pennant of her hair?

Where slightly lift her gown,
And oddly dance and let it down?

Who faints before her as she sings,
Carolling terrible, fair things?

Against whose heart does her long throat
Sob out toward morning a remote

Dim laugh?   Upon whose soul does she at last
Coldly break her body's fast

And then come quietly home, with her
Face insanely lovelier?

I never follow her nor look
To see the pathway that she took.

When she comes floating on the grass
I turn away and let her pass. . . .

I would go wholly wild were I to see
Calypso in her eyes look down at me.

PART FIVE

INSCRIPTION

For any one's clock

Here is the skeleton of time I slew,
Here is the bleak remainder of my days and nights.
Now can you resurrect my lovely Lazarus
God of all power, God of the Israelites?

HISTORY

Life's lifted heel is ever vanishing.
How bright the dust flung in our weary faces,
Who stoop to kiss the footprint on the ground
But win to no more intimate embraces.

THE LAST DEMOCRACY

The ancient and the modern dead
Sleep within the selfsame bed.
Too broad to crowd, too low to fall—
Jump in, children, room for all!

TESTIMONIAL

If there is spirit and there is flesh
And one is right and the other wrong,
Then cut me in two from brow to heel
And bury my bone, but keep my song

That says mayhap an elder erred
Who divided the body from the soul
And gave me the pieces, saying gravely,
"Never mind, death will make it whole."

A THOUGHT

Death has a horizontal house.
No one stands up in that.
Built for use and not for beauty
The lines are bare and flat.

Let once the dewy ghost of death
Drip his cold hand on you—
You are tenant in a house
With an obstructed view.

Be perpendicular your gait
And upright while you may,
For once recumbent, almost none
Rise and come away.

CERTAINTY

One thing at least have I observed,
One, if none other, life reveals—
Time pauses not to ask permission
But daily multiplies his wheels.

CALENDAR

Pale winter's mantle falls to earth, the brown Elisha
Who turns and cries with wonder in the snow,
Hearing (oh God) the chariots and horses overhead
Beneath whose mighty wheels and heels hosannah-
      flowers blow.

SNOW

Snow is humbler than most of us.
It has an elated home, an exalted birth,
Yet throws itself under man's feet
And lies down flat on the earth.

APRIL WISDOM

The rain is standing upright on the earth,
So frail a thing to be so straight and tall.
But thus erect upon its crystal heels,
Who dares to say the rain can ever fall?

EPITAPH

When death had quenched her beauty and put out
With his dark earth her perfect gaze,
She laughed aloud and with the nimble dust
Gave back her body in a cloud of praise.

EPITAPH

Earth, be light upon me.
Grave, be not too deep.
Death is too, too long a night
To pass it all in sleep.

PART SIX

SOLITUDE

I have pitched my soul
Among a solitude
Of other tents. . . .
Oh will none of you,
Will none of you
Draw back the flap
Of painted canvas?

VISION

Archangels with high foreheads and bright thighs
Pause and glimmer near me in the night.
They flare upon their quiet feet and sway
Terrible and tranquil to my sight.

Loose from your throats innumerable songs,
Angels burning at my bed,
For fear I wake in silence toward dawn,
Unangelled and uncomforted.

SONNET

For the dim moving of my earthling feet
Give me, O Lord, a taper full of light,
That I may turn upon the homeward street
From fluttering across, across the night.
How vague all living is, how vague am I
Scarcely beholding me and my own face,
Scarcely aware of my own thoughts that fly
Like moths that hover in a lonely place.
Nearer than body's flesh is God to me—
Strange that I wander then so far astray.
I have unshepherded my path and see
Myself flock with the mist and drift away.
Oh! I am pale and gaunt with sins half-sinned.
My soul droops like a flag without a wind. . . .

PRAYER

There is a burning wilderness in me,
Within this fragile territory, I.
God, like a moon, is waning and too high.
There is no nearness left in Deity.
Thus, is it thus Life teaches me to see,
To lift my eyes from myself to the sky,
To turn from my own arms wherein I lie
And kiss the swift feet of Reality?
Passionate silence, hush and make me whole,
Who daily wounded on a broken vow
Cry out as each day bleeds and takes its toll,
To be at peace! to feel, oh even now
Tranquillity alight upon my soul
Like a great bird upon a luminous bough!

II.

With Him who sets the lily on the stem,
With Him who looses summer in the loam,
With Him who wakes the winds and hushes them,
With Him who calls the dead and brings them home,
With Him the nameless, unimportunate,
The utterly within us, beautiful,
With Him I leave to-morrow and too late
Regret I left not yesterday as well.
Unto what loveliness may we commend
The desolation of the flesh that weeps,
To what untellable and bitter end
Shall wake the soul that lifts from sleep . . . and sleeps?
Oh rouse me up, good God, and keep me so,
Washing my heart in water of the snow!

ALAS, THE BIRD

Alas, the bird ascending from my spirit
Is no, not ever dove, but mute and dark.
No hush of soul or love may hope to hear it
Or follow it to eagle or to lark.
What nether Gabriel have I wooed and won,
What misty demon from a fallen sky,
That scarcely are my thoughts conceived when one
By piteous one they turn in me and die?
Some resolute Sabbath, some unearthly night,
Some midnight (pray for me) I yet may see
Under the brow of hope's heroic light
My own face like a god look down on me.
In vision's burning wake the fact will shine
Whose radiant wings once lifted will be mine.

TO ONE OF LITTLE FAITH

Put out the mourners from your heart,
And bid your still soul rise.
It is not death, but only sleep
That fastens down your eyes.

Return, O Galilean days,
Judean hands, return!
Make bloom the lily in the ash
Of this neglected urn.

HOPE INSATIATE

Feed, could I but feed at last
The almighty mystery at my breast
Day and night gnawing, crying aloud
What is this Life, who is this World?
Where is this spirit hiding in the flesh?
How to get in to the strength and the hush?
How overtake the fugitive Christ
Roaming and moonless into the dusk,
How bring him home and fasten him gleaming
So on the soul he knows no escaping?
Oh, on the hark of my listening, listening
Some word descend that will lift me!

COMMUNION

I have spoken with the dead.
From the silence of my bed
I have heard them in the night.
Their voices are as white
As altar candles.   Their voices are as gold as wheat,
And clustered in the dark their words are sweet
As ripened fruit.   Their voices are the colour of dim rain
Over grass where spring has lain.
Their speaking is an orchard of delight.
I have heard them in the night.
Their lips bloomed into heavy song
That hung like bells above me.   You are wrong
Who say the dead lie still.
I heard them sing until
The cup of silence fell in two and lay
Broken by beauty of what dead men say.

There is no loveliness I cannot see.
There is no wall too stern for me.
There is no door that can withstand
The lifted symbol of my hand.

I know an ancient shibboleth:
I pass, for I have talked with death!

ON WAKING

It is a sad thing to begin a new day
With an old pain in your heart,
Sad slowly to move your head
And stir your body in the bed,
And floating up the well of dream
Strike the light with a shock and start
A new day with an old pain in your heart.

It is a hard thing to waken
With a shadow on your mind.
Slipping from the dark breast of sleep,
Yearning to remain and keep
The broken kiss, the whole embrace,
Then hard it is to wake and find
A shadow waiting for your mind.

Love, give me light. I fall here
Returning from a better land.
Hold up the mirror to my eyes
That over my shoulder paradise
Though left behind, may shine before.
And thus deceived the soul may stand,
Haunted by heaven on every hand.

SUPPLICATION

Sing, will you let me sing, Cytherea!
Strike me not dumb with your mouth laid on my
       mouth.
Loose my song on my lips, let me be!
For a day, for a year, let me
Sing, will you let me sing, Cytherea!

Ah, the blond Cyprian, enemy, enemy!
Draw your long hands away from my hands!
Like the moon in the sky set me free.
My heart is a loud cry
Hushed by the Cyprian, ah, the blond enemy.

Hither your swans and your bright feet are burning.
I am but mortal,—immortal, let be!
If there are other gods, if there are any,
Soothe me ere dying,
Yea, on the hither side, yea, on this side of cool death!

TO A SOUL ASLEEP

Beloved, when your silences are done
And quietness has had its fill of you;
When your great days of waking are begun
And all the dead nights of your sleep are through—
Come upward, with a long torch in your hand,
Come singing, *I am free,* and make it so,
Though only God within you understand
And you yourself but hesitantly know
How much of hell you have left desolate,
How much of sorrow you have put away.
Beloved, cease from slumber.   It is late.
Behold how life, passing its urgent way,
Strikes with imperious hands upon your breast
To wake the harps that in your silence rest.

SONNET

Dark and lower darkness and gone under!
There lies the human soul in his own shadow,
There lies the brightest light gone back to pallor,
There lies the only fire fallen to cinder.
Let mend who can the glass that snaps asunder,
Let harvest, if he can, the barren meadow,
Let gather figs and silver from the willow!
O man, O woman, read the sign and ponder.
The soul brews his own season, rose or ice,
Lets down his tempests and erects his stars,
But if he try to hew a hollow tomb
And enter there to sleep while you live on,
Cry out and drive him from the fearful door,
Goad, weep and pray him from that unlit place.

CRY HARK

I have heard the wild slow horns of morning blowing
      on a hill,
I have heard the drums of dawn call up the slumbering
      light,
I have seen the crested East leap up, erect and shining.
When night the lover turns from whispering and the
      bride escapes,
Up, up between the stars she lay upon
I have seen the dawn.

I have seen the pillar of full noon standing on the
      world,
I have seen tall midday tower into the sky
And the meridian shadow cling beneath the rose.
There, there where Time and Timeless halt an instant
      face to face,
I have seen, higher and higher
Noon mounting to her golden spire.
I have seen, superb and bright,
Noon standing on her golden height.

Come slowly, yellow twilight, fill the hollow sky,
Till muted radiance of dusk possesses earth—
Now loose the vesper-moth to flutter in a bush.
Soft, soft the mellow kiss, the stealing arms of night
That draw the shadows to the mountain's breast
And lay the light to rest.

Drive home the soul into the heart, the light into the
      spirit,
Rouse, arouse us, dawn and noon! Twilight and night,
      let us not slumber!
Cry hark! the unsleeping nightingale—
Cry hark! the burning of the choral stars—
Cry hark! the implacable feet of Time pacing around the
      world!

     Until our song upon the dust is fallen stark
     And we lie down beside it in the dark,
        Cry hark!

FAITH

I will bind my broken thoughts
   With strands of water-lilies,
And go smoothly on the sand
   Bound in mighty lilies
Snaring in my heart a bird,
   Leaning on its singing.

Look!
   Flash out and walk like rain
   Across the lake.

SONG

So much wisdom needed
For this life.
Deep, oh, too deep hidden
In the dark!
Time, no time for searching
Out the answer,
  Till late, so late and longed for
  When at last
Truth opens like a door
And we run home.

FIRST THOUGHTS TO A PALINODE

Look!   This is the world, the animated earth that
      bustles among the stars,
          The earth with all her grasses
            Jumping in the wind,
          The wind about his business
            Of blowing all the trees,
          The trees with swinging shutters
            To let the birds come in,
And mountains sitting grandly on their haunches
And ocean rolling secrets phosphorescent
And desert lighted half-way up to heaven
And snow, the multitudinous, the lush, the hushed,
  And thunder.

Listen!   No reference to God or any god or myth
      electrical,
No void redone in seven days handling.   No dove.
No serpent, ah the looping liar, no Eve.
No pillared star the sky hung from that night
Oh, night no roof could roof the glory,
And the ass's eye how mother-bright.
But no more gods, born of a woman and light's
      lieutenant.
He was the Last.   Now no more.
All this gave centuries a name.   This crowns our
      blood.

But remember. The horizontal wind does his own
  blowing,
The bird that furls his flight is his own creature,
Prophetic rain alone foretells the freesia.
The lawful stars have habits no God could break.

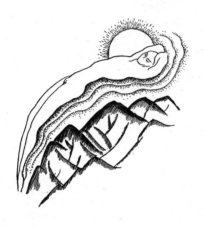

UNIT OF DESIRE

I want! I want! I want!
 —Not the moon paved on air.
I want! I want!—Not a star
 With diamond stare.

I want!—Not dreams nor visions,
 Nor bush occult with flame,
But to hear without anguish
 The sound of my own name.

Give me no fitful prophecy
 Hope-flaring at best,
But the small, specific glory
 Burning in my own breast.